SMARTER GOVERNMENT
Workbook

A 14-Week Implementation Guide to Governing for Results

Martin O'Malley

Esri Press
REDLANDS | CALIFORNIA

Esri Press, 380 New York Street, Redlands, California 92373-8100
Copyright © 2020 Esri
All rights reserved.

Printed in the United States of America
24 23 22 21 20   1 2 3 4 5 6 7 8 9 10

Library of Congress Control Number: 2019955847

ISBN (print): 9781589486027

The information contained in this document is the exclusive property of Esri unless otherwise noted. This work is protected under United States copyright law and the copyright laws of the given countries of origin and applicable international laws, treaties, and/or conventions. No part of this work may be reproduced or transmitted in any form or by any means, electronic or mechanical, including photocopying or recording, or by any information storage or retrieval system, except as expressly permitted in writing by Esri. All requests should be sent to Attention: Contracts and Legal Services Manager, Esri, 380 New York Street, Redlands, California 92373-8100, USA.

The information contained in this document is subject to change without notice.

US Government Restricted/Limited Rights: Any software, documentation, and/or data delivered hereunder is subject to the terms of the License Agreement. The commercial license rights in the License Agreement strictly govern Licensee's use, reproduction, or disclosure of the software, data, and documentation. In no event shall the US Government acquire greater than RESTRICTED/LIMITED RIGHTS. At a minimum, use, duplication, or disclosure by the US Government is subject to restrictions as set forth in FAR §52.227-14 Alternates I, II, and III (DEC 2007); FAR §52.227-19(b) (DEC 2007) and/or FAR §12.211/12.212 (Commercial Technical Data/Computer Software); and DFARS §252.227-7015 (DEC 2011) (Technical Data - Commercial Items) and/or DFARS §227.7202 (Commercial Computer Software and Commercial Computer Software Documentation), as applicable. Contractor/Manufacturer is Esri, 380 New York Street, Redlands, CA 92373-8100, USA.

@esri.com, 3D Analyst, ACORN, Address Coder, ADF, AML, ArcAtlas, ArcCAD, ArcCatalog, ArcCOGO, ArcData, ArcDoc, ArcEdit, ArcEditor, ArcEurope, ArcExplorer, ArcExpress, ArcGIS, arcgis.com, ArcGlobe, ArcGrid, ArcIMS, ARC/INFO, ArcInfo, ArcInfo Librarian, ArcLessons, ArcLocation, ArcLogistics, ArcMap, ArcNetwork, ArcNews, ArcObjects, ArcOpen, ArcPad, ArcPlot, ArcPress, ArcPy, ArcReader, ArcScan, ArcScene, ArcSchool, ArcScripts, ArcSDE, ArcSdl, ArcSketch, ArcStorm, ArcSurvey, ArcTIN, ArcToolbox, ArcTools, ArcUSA, ArcUser, ArcView, ArcVoyager, ArcWatch, ArcWeb, ArcWorld, ArcXML, Atlas GIS, AtlasWare, Avenue, BAO, Business Analyst, Business Analyst Online, BusinessMAP, CityEngine, CommunityInfo, Database Integrator, DBI Kit, EDN, Esri, esri.com, Esri–Team GIS, Esri–The GIS Company, Esri–The GIS People, Esri–The GIS Software Leader, FormEdit, GeoCollector, Geographic Design System, Geography Matters, Geography Network, geographynetwork.com, Geoloqi, Geotrigger, GIS by Esri, gis.com, GISData Server, GIS Day, gisday.com, GIS for Everyone, JTX, MapIt, Maplex, MapObjects, MapStudio, ModelBuilder, MOLE, MPS–Atlas, PLTS, Rent-a-Tech, SDE, SML, Sourcebook·America, SpatiaLABS, Spatial Database Engine, StreetMap, Tapestry, the ARC/INFO logo, the ArcGIS Explorer logo, the ArcGIS logo, the ArcPad logo, the Esri globe logo, the Esri Press logo, The Geographic Advantage, The Geographic Approach, the GIS Day logo, the MapIt logo, The World's Leading Desktop GIS, Water Writes, and Your Personal Geographic Information System are trademarks, service marks, or registered marks of Esri in the United States, the European Community, or certain other jurisdictions. CityEngine is a registered trademark of Procedural AG and is distributed under license by Esri. Other companies and products or services mentioned herein may be trademarks, service marks, or registered marks of their respective mark owners.

SMARTER GOVERNMENT

Workbook

Name

....

Representing the citizens of

....

How to use this workbook

In *Smarter Government: How to Govern for Results in the Information Age*, former governor Martin O'Malley shares his experience in successfully implementing performance management or "Stat" systems at the city and state levels in Baltimore and Maryland, respectively.

Now you can take these tested solutions and apply them to your government organization in fewer than four months. This implementation guide is your practical, hands-on companion workbook for *Smarter Government* and for realizing the promise of Stat.

A series of worksheets walks you through an easy-to-follow 14-week plan any government can use to achieve strategic performance management in three simple steps:

> **Setting up your system**

   Identify staff and resources, and set up the infrastructure you'll need to be successful at Stat.

> **Running your system**

   Set a regular cadence of accountability by running your first four departments through the Stat process.

> **Growing your system**

   Add more departments, reevaluate your goals, incorporate new technologies, and much more!

How do you start? By turning the page.

At the back of this book, you'll find a poster that highlights the basic steps you'll be taking to start Stat in your organization. It's a convenient road map for your journey toward smarter government.

Worksheets, signs, and posters in this workbook can be downloaded and printed from the Smarter Government website. Visit SmarterGovernment.com and click the "Workbook" tab.

So start. And don't stop.

The four tenets of Stat:

1. Timely, accurate information shared by all
2. Rapid deployment of resources
3. Effective tactics and strategies
4. Relentless follow-up and assessment

Introduction

Whether it is fighting crime, filling in potholes, or ensuring the trash gets picked up on time, these and a thousand other tasks are the day-to-day operations that make up the work of any city government. Now, thanks to new technologies—primarily, geographic information systems (GIS) and the Internet of Things (IoT)—these issues can all be mapped, managed, and measured with greater speed and accuracy than ever before. Government services can be delivered with greater openness and transparency than ever before. Our governments can operate with greater efficiency and effectiveness than ever before.

"Stat" refers to a performance measurement and management system invented by Jack Maple of the New York City Police Department (NYPD) in 1994, and later implemented at citywide and statewide scales and beyond.

The four tenets of any performance management regimen or Stat system—such as CompStat, CitiStat, StateStat, and others—are:

1. Timely, accurate information shared by all
2. Rapid deployment of resources
3. Effective tactics and strategies
4. Relentless follow-up and assessment

These four tenets are not endpoints. They are the beginning and the way. They are the constant framework of an ongoing search for better and more effective ways of collaborating and getting things done. The pursuit requires constant thought, intellectual curiosity, and leadership that is open to bringing forward the right questions—wherever they might lead.

In any Stat system, the GIS map plays a central, organizing role. It is not just a nice picture or another layer. The map—the geographic information map—becomes not only the integrator of once-separate silos of data, but also the field of action on which effective collaborations and winning plays can be run.

—Martin O'Malley, March 2020

Notes

Setting up your system

Setting up your system

In Silicon Valley, people who keep trying new things—even though they sometimes fail—are called innovators and entrepreneurs. In government, people who try new things and fail are fired or voted out of office. Therefore, public administration has developed a very slow, cautious, and risk-averse approach to embracing new technologies. Over the course of time, this approach has created a tyranny of "the way we have always done it" in public service.

In most big cities across America today, call centers and customer service guarantees have become the new normal. In some places, cities are combining historical data with predictive analytics to predeploy tow trucks to the places where minor accidents most frequently happen at rush hour, or deploying police patrol cars to locations represented by tiny squares on the map where crime most frequently happened during the same eight-hour shift over the previous 10 years.

This is the promise of starting Stat.

Getting started

For a successful beginning, there are primarily five trains that need to move down their respective tracks to converge by the time of your first Stat meeting. Each of them is important. They are mutually dependent upon each other. Those actions fall under the categories of **leadership commitment**, **team buy-in**, **performance data submissions**, **building the room**, and **assembling staff**.

We start, and we do not stop.

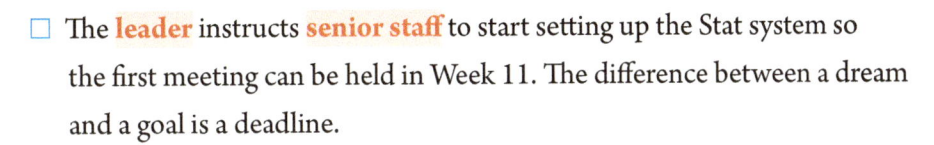

Week 1

- ☐ The **leader** instructs **senior staff** to start setting up the Stat system so the first meeting can be held in Week 11. The difference between a dream and a goal is a deadline.

- ☐ The **leader** designates one person—**the Stat director**—to be responsible for setting up and running the Stat operation and office.

- ☐ The **leader** directs every member of the **command staff** (such as the deputy mayor, finance director, city solicitor, director of IT, labor commissioner, director of human resources, etc.) to submit year-end reports of any length they choose laying out whatever key performance measures they use internally—in their own **departments'** operations—to know whether they are making progress toward their key objectives, goals, or standards of service delivery. Reports are due by Week 4.

- ☐ Together, the **senior staff** select and agree upon the appropriate space for the **Stat Room**. Proximity to the leader's office is important.

- ☐ The **leader** and **senior staff** agree on a name for the new system (e.g., CitiStat, ChicagoStat, PerformanceStat).

- ☐ One person, designated the Stat Room coordinator, takes responsibility for on-time delivery of the finished **Stat Room**.

Identify key personnel

Leader: ....

Stat director: ....

Command staff: ....

....

....

....

Senior staff: ....

....

....

....

Stat Room coordinator: ....

Other personnel: ....

....

....

....

Stat starts with leadership

The National Governors Association once asked me to share with an incoming group of Republican and Democratic governors the 10 most practical pieces of wisdom that have served me best in governing. Almost all of them were collected from other servant-leader practitioners, most who were experienced executives. Leaders can apply these pieces of wisdom across the span of government. They are important to remember when setting up your Stat system.

1. The things that get measured are the things that get done.
2. Goals and deadlines are the x-axis and y-axis of all human endeavors.
3. Small things done well make bigger things possible.
4. A graph moving in the right direction is the most beautiful achievement in self-governance. The pace of progress is variable and it's negotiable, but the direction of progress is not.
5. Effective leaders make themselves vulnerable. Own the goals of the government you run and the people you lead—no one else will.
6. Whether a large human organization moves forward to achieve meaningful goals depends in large part on whether its leaders and achievers at every level are recognized by the chief executive and by their peers.
7. Everyone must share timely, accurate information about performance and outputs—most importantly, it must be shared with the citizens you serve.
8. Communication, coordination, and collaboration are unnatural acts between nonconsenting adults. Effective leaders create and enforce data-based routines of communication, coordination, and collaboration throughout their government. These routines are the cadences of accountability that only you can set.
9. People make progress; common platforms make it possible. The geographic map of your community, city, or state is your common platform. You must base all your information systems on the map.
10. We are not here to make excuses; we are here to make progress. Repeat this mantra over and over—especially to yourself.

Small things done **well** make bigger things **possible**.

Week 2

- ☐ The **Stat director** arranges for an email to be sent to all employees throughout every department asking for any employees who are proficient in GIS, data science, and predictive analytics. Employees report back with the name, location, and contact information of any employee who answers yes. The Stat director can draw from this pool of employees when assembling their team in Week 3.

- ☐ The **leader** establishes the one common platform—**the GIS map**—to use moving forward. This GIS map becomes the operational and situational truth for the entire organization. Everybody can keep their own data however they like as long as it is open and can be displayed on the designated GIS map.

Identify employees proficient in GIS, data science, and predictive analytics

Name: ....

    Proficiency: ....

    Location: ....

    Contact info: ....

Name: ....

    Proficiency: ....

    Location: ....

    Contact info: ....

Name: ....

    Proficiency: ....

    Location: ....

    Contact info: ....

Name: ....

    Proficiency: ....

    Location: ....

    Contact info: ....

Name: ....

    Proficiency: ....

    Location: ....

    Contact info: ....

Assess your foundational tools

While a certain amount of basic IT infrastructure is necessary for implementing your Stat system, the most important step is starting and not stopping. Let the IT infrastructure catch up with you. Don't wait until you have all the technology tools—you never will. You probably already have the minimum technology required to start—GIS and spreadsheets, and maybe even an open data site—so start. And don't stop. You can add more advanced information technology tools later.

GIS

Maps and data underpin GIS, a technology that organizes information into different types of layers that can be visualized, analyzed, and combined to help us understand almost everything about our world. GIS uses maps to visualize all kinds of data layers about initiatives in our government and their impact on citizens, enabling everyone to better understand our situations, our scenarios, and our decisions.

As the foundational technology enabling any Stat system, GIS gives us the ability to model complex systems, measure performance, and see and measure what works on a scale—and with a timeliness—never before possible. Most modern governments already have GIS resources at their disposal.

Spreadsheets

Spreadsheets are a basic tool for organizing data in tabular format. You can use them to easily produce a variety of charts, graphs, and histograms. In your Stat system, they are a focal point for managing, storing, analyzing, and visualizing data and for measuring and managing performance. Spreadsheets are easily integrated with GIS, and every modern government already has access to spreadsheet software.

Open data

Open data portals are central locations where governments can store data and make it easily accessible to the public. These portals increase government transparency and accountability by providing citizens with unprecedented levels of access to their government.

If you don't already have an open data strategy, make a plan to establish one and visit data.gov/open-gov, data.un.org, and livingatlas.arcgis.com.

Stat Rooms in Baltimore and Maryland

The CompStat Room in Baltimore became the prototype for the new CitiStat Room that was soon under construction on the sixth floor of City Hall. In the year that followed, the city built several other departmental Stat Rooms in other buildings, ushering in a new way of governing across the entire City of Baltimore.

I was sworn in on December 7, 1999. The CompStat Room was completed at police headquarters by mid-January of 2000. By February, we had found the most suitable location inside City Hall to build the new CitiStat Room—the building curator's high-ceilinged space on the top floor. General Services quickly put up a wall board for the installation of a projector booth. We bolted in permanent furniture and fixtures. We mounted large, permanent projector screens on the walls. We installed computer monitors on the floor in front of the presenter and panelists. And we put blown-up versions of the service emblems, or insignia, of every major department—Fire, Police, Housing, Health, Public Works—on each of the side walls. Everything about the room said "permanent."

We found that Public Works already had a license agreement for GIS, which some members of the department used every day. That Public Works map would now serve the needs of every department as our new CitiStat map. It would now be the common platform for CitiStat.

Within 90 days, we held our first meeting. We started with Solid Waste (trash)—tangible, measurable, visible for all to see. Then, every two weeks, we added another department to the "one meeting—every two weeks" rotation. After Solid Waste, we added Water and Wastewater, then Transportation, then General Services. When those four bureaus of Public Works were rotating through in a regular repeatable routine and cadence, we added the other departments: Housing, Health, Recreation and Parks, and Fire.

Eight years later, within 90 days of my being sworn in as Governor of Maryland on January 17, 2007, we finished the new StateStat Room. Shortly after its completion, every major department began to rotate through the new performance-measured regimen. A strong, preexisting GIS map provided the common platform. New cabinet secretaries provided the new leadership, and we began our experiment anew—to see if we could accomplish this new way of governing at the more complex level of an entire state government.

Week 3

- ☐ The **department heads** deliver their **reports detailing key objectives and measures** to the **leader**.
- ☐ The **leader** prioritizes the order of **departments** to be rolled into the Stat system. Pick the low-hanging fruit—the quick wins—first. The first four departments will hold their first Stat meetings between Weeks 11 and 14.
- ☐ The Stat Room coordinator finishes the design and specifications for building the **Stat Room**. They procure furniture and assign work to internal services or the appropriate contractors. Construction should begin no later than Week 6.
- ☐ The **Stat director** assembles their team: one person with some experience in GIS and three digital natives (collectively, **analysts**) with curiosity and intelligence, ideally with some basic computer literacy and ability to manipulate spreadsheets and produce basic charts, graphs, and infographics. The analyst roles must be fully staffed by Week 7.

Assemble the Stat team

Stat director: ....

GIS analyst: ....

Analyst #1: ....

Analyst #2: ....

Analyst #3: ....

Implementation Timeline for Baltimore's CitiStat

Here's our implementation timeline for CitiStat in Baltimore from 1999 to 2005.

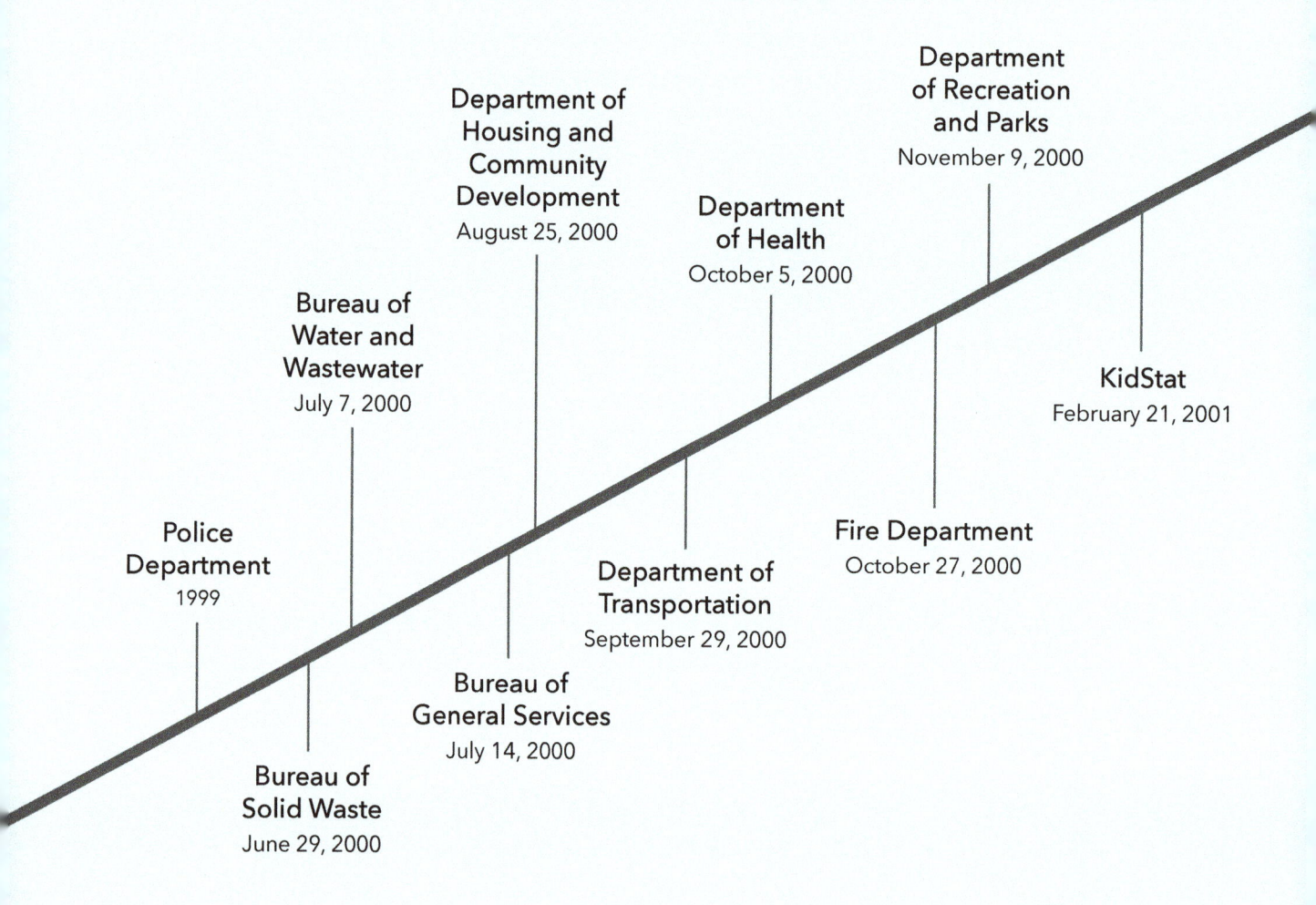

Police Department
1999

Bureau of Solid Waste
June 29, 2000

Bureau of Water and Wastewater
July 7, 2000

Bureau of General Services
July 14, 2000

Department of Housing and Community Development
August 25, 2000

Department of Transportation
September 29, 2000

Department of Health
October 5, 2000

Fire Department
October 27, 2000

Department of Recreation and Parks
November 9, 2000

KidStat
February 21, 2001

ProjectStat
May 18, 2001

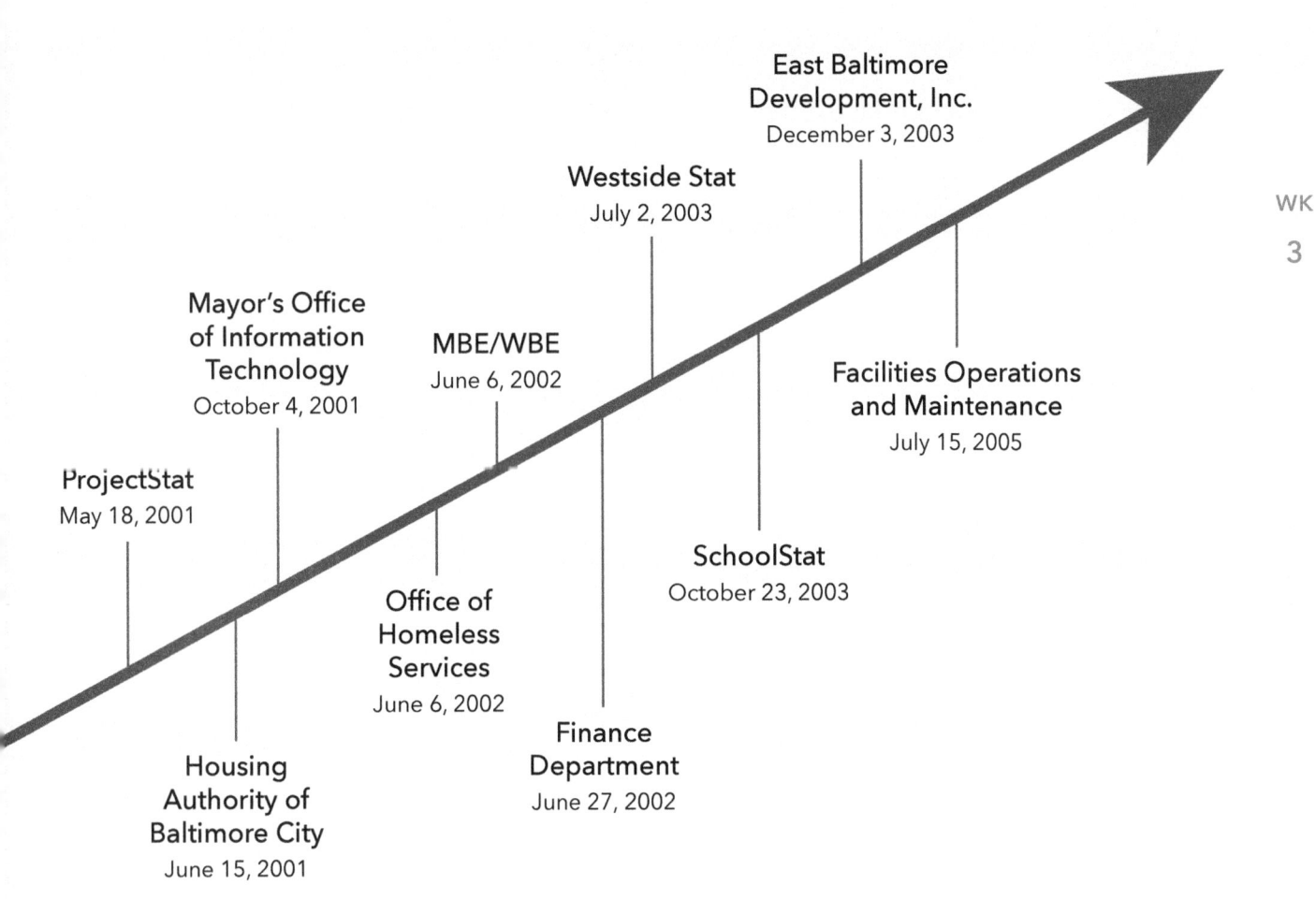

Housing Authority of Baltimore City
June 15, 2001

Mayor's Office of Information Technology
October 4, 2001

MBE/WBE
June 6, 2002

Office of Homeless Services
June 6, 2002

Finance Department
June 27, 2002

Westside Stat
July 2, 2003

SchoolStat
October 23, 2003

East Baltimore Development, Inc.
December 3, 2003

Facilities Operations and Maintenance
July 15, 2005

WK 3

Department rollout prioritization

	Department	Date of first meeting
1.		/ /
2.		/ /
3.		/ /
4.		/ /
5.		/ /
6.		/ /
7.		/ /
8.		/ /
9.		/ /
10.		/ /
11.		/ /
12.		/ /
13.		/ /
14.		/ /
15.		/ /
16.		/ /
17.		/ /
18.		/ /
19.		/ /
20.		/ /

Only the first four departments are required at this stage.

Week 4

- ☐ The **senior staff** narrow the focus of the **key performance measures** based on reports from the **departments** and the **leader**'s strategic priorities. These key performance measures will be finalized in Week 6.
- ☐ The **Stat director** begins to realign and train staff.
- ☐ The **leader** announces the date and time of the first Stat meeting, to be held in Week 11.

Identify initiatives, strategic goals, and key performance indicators

For initial departments and meetings, select a few easily understood and easily communicated successes such as eliminating a backlog (DNA analysis, food stamp applications) or a service improvement (pothole guarantee, graffiti removal, and so on).

Complete an overview of the existing performance measurement infrastructure. At a minimum, look at the monthly agency budget reports, annual budget testimony, work order reports, audits, and so on. Look for usable baselines. Tell incumbent managers: "Give us everything you use to manage your agency."

Take the results of this initial data review and juxtapose the data points against what's available from an established Stat system with an eye toward looking at gaps. If you don't track some things, but they do, probe those gaps to find deficiencies.

Meet with the existing or incoming leadership teams of the agencies prioritized for the Stat rollout to get their feedback on measures and areas of focus.

Spend a little time up front baselining financial and survey data so you can capture your improvements later. Some examples:

Initiative	Eliminate homelessness
Strategic goal	Reduce homelessness by 25 percent in 2 years
Key performance indicators	Number of homeless persons, number of homeless persons moved to housing

Initiative	Eliminate pedestrian deaths ("Vision Zero")
Strategic goal	Drive down pedestrian deaths to zero in four years
Key performance indicators	Number of pedestrian deaths, number of miles of protected bike lanes

Initiative	Reduce spending
Strategic goal	Reduce overtime by 50 percent in 1 year
Key performance indicators	Total dollars spent, number of overtime hours, number of unexcused absences

Your initiatives, strategic goals, and key performance indicators

Initiative ....

Strategic goal ....

Key performance indicators ....
....

WK 4

Initiative ....

Strategic goal ....

Key performance indicators ....
....

Initiative ....

Strategic goal ....

Key performance indicators ....
....

Initiative ....

Strategic goal ....

Key performance indicators ....
....

Identify key performance measures by department

Department   **Key performance measures***

1. ....

   ....

   ....

   ....

2. ....

   ....

   ....

   ....

3. ....

   ....

   ....

   ....

4. ....

   ....

   ....

   ....

*Possible key performance measures include budget levels by basic divisions/categories/activities within departments, staffing levels, spending year to date and month over month, women and minority business procurement spending year to date, citizen calls/requests for service, and time to delivery of service.

Week 5

- ☐ The **command staff** is given a full briefing of the Stat system with the **leader** present and with plenty of time for sharing questions, answers, fears, concerns, and hopes.

- ☐ The **leader** directs each **department head** to designate by week's end the **departmental liaison**, the single point of contact within that office who will be responsible for working on a daily basis with the **Stat director**'s team of **analysts** on data submissions and tracking of measures.

Identify key personnel for each department

Department #1: ....

    Head: ....

    Liaison: ....

Department #2: ....

    Head: ....

    Liaison: ....

Department #3: ....

    Head: ....

    Liaison: ....

Department #4: ....

    Head: ....

    Liaison: ....

The difference between a **dream** and a **goal** is a deadline.

Week 6

- [ ] The **leader** prominently mentions/brands the Stat initiative in keeping with the organization's commitment to excellence.

- [ ] The Stat system is fully staffed through a combination of reassignments and new hires.

- [ ] The **leader** schedules a time for all Stat-participating **department heads** and their **departmental liaisons** to observe an entire CompStat meeting off-site. The **leader** briefs them ahead of time, with lunch to discuss afterward.

- [ ] The **Stat director** and **senior staff** meet one-on-one with each participating **department head** to finalize the **key performance measures** for the year—lagging measures *and* leading actions. Start with the basic lagging measures—where do we want to be by end-of-year? The leading actions come into view and become more amenable to weekly and monthly measurement as time and data-driven/map-focused conversations progress.

- [ ] The Stat Room coordinator oversees the beginning of construction on the **Stat Room**.

One-on-one meetings with department heads

Department #1: ....

    Head: ....

    Date: .... / .... / ....   **Time:** .... : .... a.m./p.m.

    Location: ....

Department #2: ....

    Head: ....

    Date: .... / .... / ....   **Time:** .... : .... a.m./p.m.

    Location: ....

Department #3: ....

    Head: ....

    Date: .... / .... / ....   **Time:** .... : .... a.m./p.m.

    Location: ....

Department #4: ....

    Head: ....

    Date: .... / .... / ....   **Time:** .... : .... a.m./p.m.

    Location: ....

Building your Stat Room

In Week 6, the Stat Room coordinator begins to oversee the construction of the Stat Room. At a minimum, create seating for 50 with two large screens and a podium. Spend the money to make it permanent—wall board, projection room, installed furniture, a sign permanently bolted to the door, and so on—not just folding chairs, pop-up screens on tripods, folding tables, and other temporary solutions.

It is said that form follows function, and this is certainly true when it comes to the Stat Room. It is also said that expectations become behavior. And there is an expectation created by a proper Stat Room.

Everything about the new Stat Room should say permanent—a permanent array of desks in a horseshoe formation for the citywide police command staff; permanent projectors mounted in the ceiling; a permanent glass-enclosed booth for the staff from Planning and Research to follow the conversation and project the corresponding maps, charts, and graphs; dedicated computers; permanent big-screen monitors mounted on the walls; and a permanent podium up front where the district commander flanked by his district command staff will present—the focal point, really, of every meeting.

This room is the collaborative nerve center of your Stat system. And everything about this room should say you are in it to win, and there is no turning back.

Stat Room checklist

- ☐ Seating for 50, arrayed in a circle or U-shape
- ☐ A podium and space around or behind it for presenting teams
- ☐ Projector booth
- ☐ Dedicated computers
- ☐ Permanent ceiling-mounted projectors, and two large screens mounted permanently on the walls
- ☐ Furniture bolted to the floors
- ☐ Departmental insignia on the walls, with the organizational seal being the largest and most prominent

Observing Stat in action

On the day of our first Baltimore City Council delegation visit to the NYPD in 1999, one precinct commander and his command staff were front and center with their neighborhood maps and crime numbers behind them. In the wings, another precinct commander observed his colleagues at work: NYPD management tried to pair a more experienced, higher-performing precinct commander with a less experienced or struggling commander on the same day so that the second group could learn by listening to what was working and what was not.

CompStat is an iterative process—an ongoing, questioning dialogue held in regularly recurring intervals between emerging realities and the tactics brought forward to address them. The iterative process constantly asks the fundamental question: Is what we are doing working?

For this reason, CompStat is fundamentally entrepreneurial, not ideological. It is an ongoing, longitudinal experiment. If things work, the evidence of success would suggest that we should do more of it. If things are not working or bringing about other unintended consequences, the evidence would suggest we should stop doing it, adjust, and try something that might be more effective.

Is it working to save lives and reduce crime?

That is the daily operational question of CompStat.

As I listened to the conversation that day in New York City—watching police accountability in action—I couldn't help but wonder: "Why doesn't every police department operate this way?" And more importantly, "Why doesn't every department of every government operate this way?"

After we first implemented CitiStat in Baltimore in 2000, visitors came to see how our city reclaimed a decrepit waterfront and turned it into a tourist attraction. As our administration progressed, mayors and mayoral candidates from other cities started coming to Baltimore to see and understand CitiStat. Our distinguished American visitors included public administrators from state, local, and federal governments. And frequently, we had visitors from around the world—shepherded sometimes by our U.S. State Department or Vice President Al Gore's National Partnership for Reinventing Government.

As CitiStat continued to gain traction in Baltimore, an interesting thing happened: officials from across the country and even as far as Europe and Asia—from townships, cities, states, and even federal agencies—began sending people to learn more about CitiStat. Their interest was not surprising.

Notes

WK 6

STAT OFFICE

Working toward Smarter Government

Week 7

- ☐ The **leader** sends a calendar of all Stat meetings scheduled *for the next 12 months* to all participating **department heads** and their senior staff. The accompanying note advises that participation and attendance is mandatory and to adjust their schedules moving forward accordingly.

- ☐ The newly hired **analysts** start working out of one office. Each analyst is assigned two **departments** to consistently shepherd, guide, serve, and push. A "**Stat Office**" nameplate is prominently displayed on the office door (see facing page and SmarterGovernment.com/workbook).

Assign analysts to departments

Analyst #1: ....

    Department: ....

    Department: ....

Analyst #2: ....

    Department: ....

    Department: ....

Analyst #3: ....

    Department: ....

    Department: ....

Stat staff (compiled from pages 6, 13, 16, 21, and 29)

Leader: ....

Stat director: ....

Stat Room coordinator: ....

GIS analyst: ....

Senior staff: ....

....

....

Department #1	Department #2
Name:	Name: ....
Head:	Head: ....
Liaison:	Liaison: ....
Analyst:	Analyst: ....
Staff:	Staff: ....
....	....
....	....
....	....
....	....

Command staff: ....

....

....

....

Other staff: ....

....

....

WK
7

Department #3	Department #4
Name:	Name: ....
Head:	Head: ....
Liaison:	Liaison: ....
Analyst:	Analyst: ....
Staff:	Staff: ....
....	....
....	....
....	....
....	....

The things that get **measured** are the things that get **done**.

Week 8

☐ The **Stat director** and the team of **analysts** meet with each **department** for an informal run-through of issues to be discussed at the tabletop dry runs to be held in Weeks 9 and 10. They examine and resolve or assign deadlines to any critical issues remaining regarding data collection, timely submission, or geographic display.

Schedule informal run-throughs

Department #1: ....

    Date: ..../......../........ **Time:** ....:........ a.m./p.m.

    Location: ....

    Issues: ....

    ....

Department #2: ....

    Date: ..../......../........ **Time:** ....:........ a.m./p.m.

    Location: ....

    Issues: ....

    ....

Department #3: ....

    Date: ..../......../........ **Time:** ....:........ a.m./p.m.

    Location: ....

    Issues: ....

    ....

Department #4: ....

    Date: ..../......../........ **Time:** ....:........ a.m./p.m.

    Location: ....

    Issues: ....

    ....

STAT ROOM

Working toward Smarter Government

Week 9

- ☐ The Stat Room coordinator oversees the completion of the **Stat Room**. A "Stat Room" nameplate is prominently displayed on the door (see facing page and SmarterGovernment.com/workbook).

- ☐ Tabletop dry runs of the **first and second departments' data submissions and operational presentations** are held. These are held as two separate meetings, preferably back to back. Use basic SWOT analysis—strengths, weaknesses, opportunities, threats. Knowing the **department heads'** priorities, ask which three areas they believe should be the focus of their upcoming hour at the first meeting. The seated conversation around this conference table should be used to prepare and give confidence to departmental teams for their first Stat meetings to be held in Weeks 11 and 12.

Schedule tabletop dry runs

Department #1: ....

Date: .... / .... / .... **Time:** .... : .... a.m. / p.m.

Location: Stat Room

Department #2: ....

Date: .... / .... / .... **Time:** .... : .... a.m. / p.m.

Location: Stat Room

WK 9

SWOT analysis

Department: ....

Strengths	Weaknesses

Opportunities	Threats

Which three areas should be the focus of the first meeting?

1. ....

   ....

2. ....

   ....

3. ....

   ....

Week 10

☐ Hold the same type of tabletop dry runs as Week 9, this time with the **third and fourth departments**' **data submissions and operational presentations**. Again, hold one separate meeting for each department, and use basic SWOT analysis. Knowing the **department heads**' priorities, ask which three areas they believe should be the focus of their upcoming hour at their first Stat meetings to be held in Weeks 13 and 14.

Schedule tabletop dry runs

Department #3: ....

Date: .... / .... / .... **Time:** .... : .... a.m./p.m.

Location: Stat Room

Department #4: ....

Date: .... / .... / .... **Time:** .... : .... a.m./p.m.

Location: Stat Room

Summary

In Weeks 1 through 10, you set up all the infrastructure you needed to run a successful Stat system—identifying key personnel, prioritizing departments for rollout, building the Stat Room, etc.

In Weeks 11 through 14, you'll run your first four departments through your Stat system and be well on your way to smarter government.

Running
your system

Running your system

Most governments monitor their performance at annual budget reviews—if they track performance at all. With CitiStat, we monitored departmental performance biweekly. With StateStat, we monitored agency performance monthly, and in some cases bimonthly, identifying data trends before they turned into problems. Through relentless follow-up with our agencies, we ensured that the solutions we crafted together were not only implemented efficiently and quickly but were effective in turning the data trends back in the right direction.

In Weeks 11 to 14, you'll roll out Stat meetings for your first four departments.

Schedule your first four departments

	Tuesday	
	9:00-10:00 a.m.	10:15-11:15 a.m.
Week 11	Department #1:	
Week 12	Department #2:	
Week 13	Department #1:	Department #3:
Week 14	Department #2:	Department #4:

Week 11

- ☐ The first Stat meeting with the **first department** takes place from 9 a.m. to 10 a.m. on Tuesday. Their second meeting will happen in two weeks, during Week 13. Same time, same place.
- ☐ Identify **key staff** using the provided name tent templates (see page 48 and SmarterGovernment.com/workbook).
- ☐ **Analysts** prepare post-meeting reports and follow up with their assigned **departmental liaisons**.

Week 11	Department #1:	
Week 12	Department #2:	
Week 13	Department #1:	Department #3:
Week 14	Department #2:	Department #4:

Stat meeting checklist

- ☐ Have standard templates in place
- ☐ Have an agenda
- ☐ Start on time
- ☐ The leader establishes a collaborative and open tone
- ☐ Don't forget the maps
- ☐ Finish on time

Stat meeting agenda

Department: ....

Date: ..../......../........

Time: ......:...... a.m./p.m. to ......:...... a.m./p.m. (one hour)

Location: Stat Room

Agenda:	Strategic goal #1
	• Progress toward goal
	Strategic goal #2
	• Progress toward goal
	Strategic goal #3
	• Progress toward goal
	Address specific problems
	• New tactics
	• New strategies
	• New leading actions
	• New performance measures

Holding your first meeting

The Stat meeting process consists of several repeatable routines for convening and focusing the attention of the group on the most leading actions that drive you to achieve strategic goals.

Set aside one hour per department or agency to figure out root causes or to discuss or imagine new tactics and strategies for dealing with the big persistent problems. For example:

- "Why was the tree contract so hard to manage?" "Because the scope of work was so broad and inclusive, people didn't know what they were actually bidding on, so there were huge overruns and add-ons."
- "Why was the procurement drawn so broadly?" "Because we have a huge backlog, and we need help."
- "Why is the backlog so large—what type of complaint/task is the major driver of the backlog?" "We will look at the biggest problem in the backlog and put out a new RFP for that portion of the work."

Develop standard templates

For every department and meeting, use standard spreadsheet templates to record data indicating progress on a variety of performance measures. Budget numbers are often the first easy successes, because most government agencies are far more adept at telling you what government spends than they are about what government does or how well it does it.

Especially at the outset, be wary of falling into the trap of trying to measure *everything*. Focus on the "primary colors" of performance for any given department—those monthly indicators that together paint a clear picture of operational progress. Over time, you'll get better at focusing on the leading actions that improve performance.

And whatever you measure, make sure that it lands on the map.

Separate departmental silos of information will all be forced to land on the same map. This allows you to see where the problems are and where your money and efforts are landing. You will see where your problems are clustered or concentrated; which teams of city workers are performing at a high level, and which are not; and which neighborhoods are being well served, and which are not. You will be able to identify patterns and get inside the turning radius of the problem.

Using departmental templates

The first several lines of the new departmental spreadsheets for CitiStat in Baltimore were fairly standard across all departments. Line one was dollars spent with minority- and women-owned businesses on a year-to-date basis. (We made it the first line intentionally because we had the most ambitious goals in the nation. We also had never before hit our goals, but soon we would.) The next lines were the amount of budgeted dollars spent on a year-to-date basis. These lines were followed by the data on unexcused work absences, and its related cousin, dollars spent on overtime year to date.

For the budget numbers, we could see the spending on a year-to-date basis and compare the rate of spending to the same date of the prior year. This visibility allowed everyone to see whether we were overspending or underspending on our budgets. But for other outcome metrics, we were starting from scratch, and we had to develop month-over-month and year-to-date comparisons as time, experience, and the measuring of progress moved forward.

After these initial budget, procurement, and personnel metrics, we tracked the performance measures of the unique missions of the individual departments. In a collaborative way, we worked with the experienced staff of each department to tease out the best measures of effectiveness and performance. For the Health Department, it could be the number of addicted people currently in treatment or the number of children immunized against disease. For Recreation and Parks, it could be the number of children participating in recreation center activities. For Transportation, it could be potholes and curb repairs.

Before the meeting

Agencies submit customized data templates each month. The Stat team analyzes the data to identify trends, conducts site visits, and meets with agency staff to evaluate programs. The analysts turn this into executive briefs that are shared with the Stat panel, including the leader, before each meeting.

The agenda you set should be a combination of a stocktake agenda (i.e., give us updates on these six lagging indicators for your department) as well as a problem-solving agenda (i.e., today we are going to have a discussion about developing new tactics, strategies, or leading actions for dealing with a specific problem).

And don't forget the maps! Place matters, and district-by-district bar graphs can often be more intuitively understood with shade maps or heat maps or even pin maps during the meeting. Especially in the area of service delivery, it's crucial to maintain geographic integrity and accountability with the scoreboard displayed on a map that everyone can understand.

Outline for a department executive brief

To:	Leader Stat director Command staff Senior staff Department head Department staff Et al.
Date:	......../......../........
From:	Stat analyst
Department:	....
Subject:	Executive brief for the reporting period of ..../......../........ to ..../......../........
Key objectives:	Current trends Initiative updates
Goal review:	Strategic goal #1: Progress toward goal Strategic goal #2: Progress toward goal Strategic goal #3: Progress toward goal
Attached:	Data observations on progress toward strategic goals along with suggested lines of inquiry

WK 11

During the meeting

Important success factors in holding a Stat meeting include:

- The leader's presence and his or her expression of confidence and commitment to the director and the new collaborative routine.
- A collaborative and open tone set by leadership—not just a small accomplishment but crucial.
- A prompt start.
- The preparation in terms of the display of data for all to see— it's no small feat to get everyone to make timely submissions.

The director leads the Stat panel, which includes the leader, chief of staff, legal counsel, and staff from the departments being reviewed. The panel questions agency leaders on the trends identified in the executive briefs and works with these leaders to develop solutions. Agencies bring a variety of staff to the table, including their secretary and deputy secretaries, human resources, finance, and program staff to assist in the discussion. Stat meetings are innately collaborative—not only does the panel ask questions of the agency but the agency uses the time to ask for assistance or guidance from the leader, senior staff, legal counsel, other relevant departments, and so on.

It's important that the entire departmental team hears the conversations and brings the urgency and focus back to the organization. It's also important that they sit behind the presenter, so you can read their faces and call on them when it's obvious that one of them has a different operational perspective to share.

After the meeting

The Stat analysts prepare comprehensive follow-up reports for the agencies detailing the action items discussed in the meeting, as well as any other questions or concerns. The agencies complete and submit the follow-up reports prior to the next Stat meeting. The analysts work continuously with their agencies throughout the period between meetings to ensure progress is being made quickly and efficiently.

To support the goals of transparency and open government, the Stat team posts comprehensive meeting summaries online, including all data and charts used in the analysis. The team keeps an executive dashboard updated and prominently displayed on your website so citizens can see the measures you are watching. This dashboard allows citizens to view and interact with the data anytime through your open data portal and track the progress toward your strategic goals.

In the spirit of true openness and accountability, every report generated for a Stat meeting should be treated as a public document and shared on your open data site. This sharing also applies to all data, maps, infographics, dashboards, and other supporting resources.

WK
11

Working toward **Smarter Government**

Start and don't stop.

Name

Stat Director

Week 12

- ☐ The second Stat meeting, the first with the **second department**, takes place from 9 a.m. to 10 a.m. This department's second meeting will take place in two weeks, during Week 14. Same time, same place.
- ☐ **Analysts** prepare post-meeting reports and follow up with their assigned **departmental liaisons**.

Week 11	Department #1:	
Week 12	Department #2:	
Week 13	Department #1:	Department #3:
Week 14	Department #2:	Department #4:

Notes

Week 13

- ☐ The **first department** returns at 9 a.m. for their one hour of focus, collaboration, and mutual accountability. They are followed by the first Stat meeting by the **third department** from 10:15 a.m. to 11:15 a.m. in the same space. Rapid turnover of room is intentional.
- ☐ **Analysts** prepare post-meeting reports and follow up with their assigned **departmental liaisons**.

Week 11	Department #1:	
Week 12	Department #2:	
Week 13	Department #1:	Department #3:
Week 14	Department #2:	Department #4:

We are not here to make **excuses**; we are here to make **progress**.

Week 14

- ☐ The **second department** returns at 9 a.m. for their second Stat meeting. They are followed by the first meeting with the **fourth department** from 10:15 a.m. to 11:15 a.m. in the same space; again, rapid turnover is intentional.
- ☐ **Analysts** prepare post-meeting reports and follow up with their assigned **departmental liaisons**.

Week 11	Department #1:	
Week 12	Department #2:	
Week 13	Department #1:	Department #3:
Week 14	Department #2:	Department #4:

Setting a cadence of accountability

A key feature of the Stat system is regularly scheduled meetings (typically bi-weekly at the city level; once a month or bimonthly at the county, state, or multi-jurisdictional level), where personnel present summaries of statistics and maps to agency leadership. This schedule allows the executives to review performance, set strategy, and hold individual agencies accountable for good—or bad—results.

Example biweekly meeting schedule for 16 departments

Week	Tuesday (a.m.) 9:00-10:00	Tuesday (a.m.) 10:15-11:15	Wednesday (a.m.) 9:00-10:00	Wednesday (a.m.) 10:15-11:15	Thursday (a.m.) 9:00-10:00	Thursday (a.m.) 10:15-11:15	Friday (a.m.) 9:00-10:00	Friday (a.m.) 10:15-11:15
11	Dept. #1							
12	Dept. #2							
13	Dept. #1	Dept. #3						
14	Dept. #2	Dept. #4						
15	Dept. #1	Dept. #3	Dept. #5					
16	Dept. #2	Dept. #4	Dept. #6					
17	Dept. #1	Dept. #3	Dept. #5	Dept. #7				
18	Dept. #2	Dept. #4	Dept. #6	Dept. #8				
19	Dept. #1	Dept. #3	Dept. #5	Dept. #7	Dept. #9			
20	Dept. #2	Dept. #4	Dept. #6	Dept. #8	Dept. #10			
21	Dept. #1	Dept. #3	Dept. #5	Dept. #7	Dept. #9	Dept. #11		
22	Dept. #2	Dept. #4	Dept. #6	Dept. #8	Dept. #10	Dept. #12		
23	Dept. #1	Dept. #3	Dept. #5	Dept. #7	Dept. #9	Dept. #11	Dept. #13	
24	Dept. #2	Dept. #4	Dept. #6	Dept. #8	Dept. #10	Dept. #12	Dept. #14	
25	Dept. #1	Dept. #3	Dept. #5	Dept. #7	Dept. #9	Dept. #11	Dept. #13	Dept. #15
26	Dept. #2	Dept. #4	Dept. #6	Dept. #8	Dept. #10	Dept. #12	Dept. #14	Dept. #16
27	Dept. #1	Dept. #3	Dept. #5	Dept. #7	Dept. #9	Dept. #11	Dept. #13	Dept. #15
28	Dept. #2	Dept. #4	Dept. #6	Dept. #8	Dept. #10	Dept. #12	Dept. #14	Dept. #16

Other tasks

- [ ] Concentrate on getting better every week by focusing on the four tenants of Stat: timely, accurate information shared by all; more rapid deployment of resources; ever more effective tactics and strategies; and relentless follow-up throughout ever-deeper levels of government.

- [ ] Make sure all **data submissions** from **departments** are delivered to the **Stat director** by noon two business days *before* each meeting. Strictly enforce this from the start—it needs to become as routine as brushing your teeth, combing your hair, or cutting your grass. It is the *foundational* repeatable routine.

- [ ] Every meeting should have a three- to four-page executive brief laying out the three to five main topics for each meeting with time allotments for each topic along with **key graphs or measures**. The more comprehensive data template should follow the brief as an attachment.

- [ ] Follow-up briefs should be in *all* **participants**' inboxes with any recipient's personal responsibility for follow-through highlighted on the subject line.

WK
14

Executive brief template

Department: ....

Date: .... / .... / ....   **Time:** .... : .... a.m. / p.m.

Data submitted? Yes / No

Main topics:
1. ....
   ....

2. ....
   ....

3. ....
   ....

4. ....
   ....

5. ....
   ....

Lessons from CitiStat

Did I attend every CitiStat meeting? Yes, at first. Over time, I personally attended fewer meetings. But I figured out ways to somehow be present at every one.

The CitiStat Room was designed as a semicircle, with the department head at a podium flanked on either side by her or his command staff and the mayor facing them on the other side of the semicircle flanked by my command staff.

My command staff included cabinet members whose duties, like my own, were cross-functional and enterprise-wide. Some cities referred to this group as the "executive cabinet." They included the finance director, city solicitor, labor commissioner, human resources director, and head of information technology. Leading the discussion every week was the CitiStat director and/or my first deputy mayor. Depending on the subject matter being discussed, one of the other three deputy mayors would also be at the CitiStat table.

The news media had a hard time understanding the collaborative nature of CitiStat, comparing meetings to a mayoral firing squad for bad department heads. For us, it was a repeatable routine that kept us focused on our mission. It was a precious hour every two weeks to focus on the vital functions of one department. The sharper departmental leaders soon realized it was an opportunity for them to let me and my command staff know how we could better support them in their jobs.

It was a time for leaders to rise.

At every meeting, each of us had a copy of an agenda laying out the major areas for discussion. The department head would stand at a podium with the graphs, maps, and numbers measuring their department's performance projected onto large screens behind them. Also on the screen was a photo of the department head, bureau chief, or manager who owned the numbers on the screen—so everyone could see which leader was responsible for what performance.

The beginning questions—on any topic, really—were always the same: Are we doing better over these two weeks than the two weeks before? If not, why not? And how can we improve?

These meetings were not a firing squad, and they were not a cross-examination—although, sometimes tough cross-examination was required to get to the heart of the operational challenge. It was first and foremost a conversation about how we could better collaborate to improve performance. Mapping the problems and collecting the numbers helped us understand how well we were serving the people we worked for.

Summary

In Weeks 11 through 14, you successfully ran your first four departments through your new Stat system.

In Weeks 15 and beyond, you'll grow your system by adding more departments, adjusting and adding new goals, incorporating new technologies and methods, and more.

Growing
your system

Growing your system

Weeks 15+

The most important step in implementing your Stat system is starting and not stopping. Not many administrations have the intestinal fortitude to persevere. Keep going. Grow your system, and you will increasingly deliver better and better results for your citizens.

- ☐ Add more **departments** to your rotation of Stat meetings.
- ☐ As you begin to meet and even exceed your strategic goals, continually re-evaluate and add more goals.
- ☐ Expand your IT infrastructure to include things beyond GIS maps and spreadsheets such as executive dashboards, 311 for customer service, and ArcGIS Hub.
- ☐ Discover new sources of data, build new relationships, and prepare for emergencies by performing data drills.
- ☐ Incorporate new technologies and methods, such as sensors and alerts, predictive analytics, and artificial intelligence.

Do not lose sight of the whole; better choices are possible when they are guided by more holistic measures of the common good we share.

Add more departments

In "Setting up your system" in Week 3, you made a list of departments and prioritized their rollout in the Stat system. Work through your priority list and add more departments at a reasonably aggressive rate.

Schedule rollout of additional departments

Day of week: ....

	9:00-10:00 a.m.	10:15-11:15 a.m.
Week 15	Department #5:	
Week 16	Department #6:	
Week 17	Department #5:	Department #7:
Week 18	Department #6:	Department #8:

WK
15+

Continually reevaluate your goals

A strategic goal met is not an end; it is an opportunity to do even better. If your strategic goal is to reduce homelessness by 25 percent and you meet that goal, set an even more aggressive goal. After all, your ultimate goal is to *eliminate* homelessness, not just reduce it by a certain percentage.

Likewise, a strategic goal *not* met is equally an opportunity for reevaluation and resetting. Maybe your goal was too aggressive and unrealistic. Then again—and more likely—maybe your goal was on point but your tactics to meet that goal were unsuccessful. Instead of lowering your expectations, modify your tactics.

Expand your IT infrastructure

More advanced technologies you can add to your IT infrastructure as your Stat system expands and becomes more sophisticated include such things as executive dashboards, 311 for customer service, and ArcGIS Hub.

Executive dashboards

Set up an executive dashboard for leadership that gives instant real-time visibility into such things as operational delivery, fiscal health/spending, and public sentiment. Government leaders now commonly use executive dashboards to proactively view critical metrics, identify trends, raise questions, and devise new management strategies. Dashboards can be deployed by governments and used by decision-makers on mobile and tablet devices as well as desktop computers.

Executive dashboards offer map-based views of key performance indicators that leaders, decision-makers, and senior management need to effectively run an organization. They aggregate information from multiple sources and serve as a starting point from which the leaders and other executives can get a sense of the big picture before digging deeper into data. Dashboards can be used to view performance across an entire jurisdiction or to drill down to a specific neighborhood of interest.

Building on the innovation and legacy of CompStat, state-of-the-art dashboard apps today provide a variety of ways to interact with data and visualize patterns in your community.

Design your own executive dashboard

Department: ....

Strategic goal: ....

Key performance indicators					
#1	#2	#3	#4	#5	#6

What do you want the map to show?

....

....

....

WK
15+

63

311 for customer service

In Baltimore, one of our most important innovations—complementing CitiStat—was an idea we borrowed from the City of Chicago.

The idea was to have one phone number, with trained call takers, for every type of service for which a citizen might call. Seems simple. It was the same way 911 had been helping police and fire respond to service calls for decades. But in 1999, the idea of applying 911-level service to all citizen calls was new. Only Chicago, under Mayor Richard Daley, had done it.

In the old days, council members gave out jumbo cards at community meetings listing 300 different phone numbers. Trash problem? Look under "T." Dead tree? Look under "D"—and you had better have your glasses handy for the fine print.

Typically, city employees who answered such calls had not earned the assignment because of their excellent phone manners. Too often they were problem employees that could not be trusted out in the field. Managers stuck them inside where they could keep an eye on them—answering phone calls from our customers and bosses—the citizens. It should not have been surprising that calls were sometimes dropped, handled poorly, and handled rudely. And we wondered why citizens were angry.

We borrowed from Chicago's pioneering work and in 2001 became the second big city in America to implement a single customer service call center: Dial 311 for all city services. Along with the call center was the ability—just like 911—to monitor dispatch and delivery of service. For the first time, every citizen could now receive an individual customer service number for tracking their service request to delivery and a time frame (a deadline) within which to expect the service to be completed. Add to that a courteous call taker, and it was a huge winner with citizens.

We called it CitiTrack. The ability to independently monitor service requests and the timeliness of their delivery was a powerful pipeline of evidence that came to inform every CitiStat meeting. CitiTrack not only informed the decisions of the second new tenet of city government—rapid deployment of resources—CitiTrack also informed every tenet from timely and accurate information shared by all, to the effectiveness of our tactics and strategies, to the relentlessness of our follow-up.

People make progress; **common platforms** make it possible.

ArcGIS Hub

No one cares about a neighborhood as much as the people who live in it. Residents and citizens want to engage with government to understand policies, share their local knowledge, and improve their communities. They have a tremendous opportunity to use modern technology, combined with the collective knowledge of governments, citizens, and researchers, to build smarter communities.

How do smarter communities around the world encourage effective governments to work closely with residents, and vice versa? All facets of policymaking, people, processes, and technology must be in balance and aligned to make engagement efforts honest, supported, and successful. So while innovative technology can dramatically improve citizens' access to government and the overall success of such partnerships, it must be deployed in a way that supports shared outcomes.

ArcGIS Hub is a new, two-way engagement platform that connects government and citizens. It introduces a new framework designed to prioritize initiatives, organize data and teams, measure the progress of key performance indicators, and empower the community to understand complex relationships with explorative analytics and infographic reports. ArcGIS Hub includes tools for managing open data, but it goes beyond just open data. It provides a catalyst for creating smarter communities.

ArcGIS Hub initiatives are focused, policy-driven goals that result from executive and strategic objectives. Vision Zero, for example, is a global initiative to prevent traffic-related deaths and life-altering injuries. The goal—to have zero traffic-related deaths—is clearly identifiable as an important and measurable metric. Everyone has a vested interest in accomplishing this target, and as a result, groups are motivated and focused on how they can work together to achieve this outcome.

In addition to aiming data and apps at a specific goal, ArcGIS Hub initiatives can help governments better coordinate their own work and invite other organizations, such as civic advocacy groups, to cohost events, gather new data, perform analysis, and collaborate with tech developers to devise creative solutions to issues. ArcGIS Hub conversations capture discussion and feedback from the community. These forums track public feedback, government responses, and ArcGIS Hub initiative team actions to ensure that everyone is working together toward the initiative's goal. For more information, visit esri.com/hub.

Example ArcGIS Hub initiatives:

- Address homelessness
- Increase trust in policing
- Combat vector-borne disease
- Reduce pedestrian deaths
- Make parking easier
- Increase affordable housing
- Attract business to community
- Fight opioid addiction

ArcGIS Hub
SIMPLY CONNECTING CITIZENS AND GOVERNMENT

Define your own initiatives:

ArcGIS Hub
SIMPLY CONNECTING CITIZENS AND GOVERNMENT

WK
15+

67

Perform data drills

A data drill is a multiorganization collaboration exercise used to gain greater insight into how a city collectively thinks about, manages, shares, and uses data. During a drill, we discover data and build relationships, so people who are responding to an emergency have access to "data at the speed of thought."

Generally, data drills are developed and conducted based on some operational challenge that involves data and requires multiorganizational cooperation to achieve a desired result. Drills can be designed for (but are not limited to):

- Specific scenarios (hurricane flood zones, homeless counts, data center disruption)
- Capacity building (collecting data, learning how to operationalize a specific dataset)
- Operations development (two agencies cleaning up downed trees in a joint operation)
- Testing software (testing new features in a data-sharing platform)

Data drills are meant to help us take on that challenge by having organizations across the city surfacing, sharing, and integrating data. A drill takes place over a designated period, with a specified start time and end time. It forces all the participants to work within similar time constraints that we tend to see in real life. Every data drill results in overall citywide data IQ growing ever so slightly.

Data drill deliverables should be defined early in the planning phase. They might include (but are not limited to):

- Identification of datasets, with metadata and data dictionaries
- An organization-specific operational workflow relevant to data and use cases
- Interagency workflow for operations, analysis, and network infrastructure
- List of organization contacts, roles, and responsibilities
- Documentation of activities and observations
- Report, with recommendations

Incorporate new technologies and methods

Sensors and alerts

Smarter governments use modern technologies—like big data, GIS, and the IoT—to make their cities more inclusive, prosperous, resilient, and sustainable. They use these modern technologies to tackle their biggest operational, social, and environmental challenges and use big data and big data analytics to solve them.

Enter the wild world of sensors and alerts—our newfound ability to monitor, in real time, the dynamics of a city through the deployment of electronic sensors. What kind of sensors?

Sensors—powered by small solar panels—that alert city cleaning crews when a public trash can needs emptying. Audio sensors that can instantaneously pinpoint—with accuracy and certainty—the exact location where a gunshot has been fired. Sensors that monitor the value of green infrastructure—like porous alleyways and rain gardens—for the absorption of stormwater that would otherwise poison streams. Sensors that monitor traffic flows to reduce congestion and turn traffic control lights into dynamic systems that optimize the flow of cars. Sensors that measure air pollution and its concentrations across a city.

Motion sensors, like the ones deployed in Singapore, that protect the well-being of senior citizens living alone. Sensors in ankle bracelets that make sure vulnerable children on juvenile probation are obeying their curfews and not hanging out on dangerous corners where gunfire flies.

Carnegie Mellon University worked with the city to deploy low-cost and highly accurate sensors across the many bridges that span the three rivers of Pittsburgh.

Another team of engineers is working on the technology of sensors that ride on the city's fleet of vehicles and relay a nonstop flow of data on the conditions of the roads and bridges over which they travel.

Doing something about what we know is still the key, but sensors are giving us a whole new way to know—and at a scale and speed never before possible.

Of course, smartphones in the hands of caring citizens are a pretty powerful feedback loop, as well. But automated sensors are a new and more cost-effective way to better manage moving things.

WK
15+

Predictive analytics

Shortly after the attacks of September 11, I had occasion as mayor to sit down for a frank discussion about information sharing (or more exactly, the lack of it) between local, state, and federal law enforcement. One of the career federal intelligence officials at the table said, "If we only knew what we already know…"

Predictive analytics is the ability to understand what we already know. It is the science of probabilities—based on past experience—applied to present and future events. Predicting where structural fires are most likely to happen, where food-borne illnesses are most likely to strike, which neighborhoods are most likely to flood, or where abandoned and vacant housing is most likely to cluster.

With predictive analytics, the science of *where* meets the science of *why*—when we understand what happened where, why, and…when *before*.

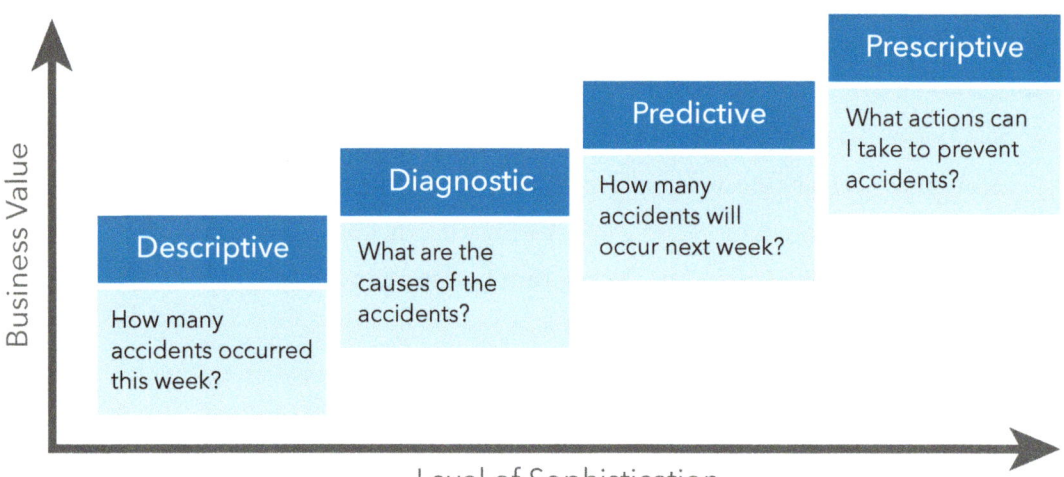

What do we mean by "predictive analytics"? This model from the management consulting firm Grant Thornton, LLP, lays out the evolutionary progression in the sophistication and the value of predictive analytics. In this case, the goal is determining how to reduce traffic accidents.

Artificial intelligence

The emergence of artificial intelligence (AI) is another crucial technological advancement for governing our cities, counties, states, and countries. AI uses advanced computing techniques to enable computers to discern and understand patterns in ways that people gathered around a Stat meeting might. But the computer potentially can do this work faster and with a deeper memory.

How might AI be integrated into future Stat systems? Marc Benioff, CEO of Salesforce, holds weekly meetings with executives and senior staff to review goals and measure progress. One seat at that conference table is reserved for Salesforce's AI software, named Einstein. Einstein has access to all the company's data, including sales numbers, and is frequently called on not only to verify information presented by other participants in the meeting, but also to provide deeper insights.

It's hard for me to imagine a similar AI bot sitting at the table during a reinstituted CitiStat meeting in Baltimore.

Sadly, in today's reality, when department heads quit or get fired or administrations change, a lot of institutional memory gets wiped away. Maybe AI Stat bots could save us from that inevitable brain drain. Not only would an AI Stat bot have access to data about the performance metrics and customer service requests of the current administration, but it would also have a deep library of knowledge that goes back in time—well beyond the collective memory of any current assortment of administrators and department leaders.

The AI Stat bot would know which work crews had their highest performance levels, when, and under which leaders. It would know what has been done in the past, what worked, and what didn't work. The internet would allow it to network with other AI Stat bots. These Stat bots might be in the employment of other cities or states across the country—all of them working on real-life problems in real time on real maps.

The AI Stat bot might access the knowledge and experience of other cities that have successfully tackled homelessness, drug addiction, or lead poisoning. It might help everybody make better decisions based on a much larger pool of real-world experiences and better data.

Do not lose sight of the whole

The philosopher Pierre Teilhard de Chardin, S.J., once said, "It is the law of all progress that it is made by passing through some stages of instability."

In many ways, we postindustrial people like to think of ourselves as pro-growth. We believe in growing jobs and growing opportunity. We believe in children growing healthy, growing educated, and growing strong. We believe in grandparents growing old with dignity, security, and love. Increasingly of late, we believe in growing more trees, growing sustainable fisheries, and growing food locally to feed our citizens. And, as Americans, we still believe in growing prosperity for every generation.

In our state, we measured the value of higher education, the cost of crime, income inequality, the cost of ozone depletion, the value of volunteer work, and score of other indicators—from clean air to healthier waters. There were, in all, 26 quality-of-life measures spanning economic, social, and environmental progress.

In city after city, mayors and others are instituting a citizen happiness index to gauge public satisfaction with city living.

Biologist and author Janine Benyus once said, "Life creates conditions conducive to life." Today, we have within our power—as cities, as states, as communities, as individuals—the ability to achieve rising standards of living, better-educated children, more affordable college, a more highly skilled American workforce, safer neighborhoods, a safer and more resilient homeland, healthier people, and a more sustainable way of life with the other living systems of the earth.

But this will not happen on its own.

Leadership is important. Broader understanding is essential. Progress is a choice. And better choices are possible when they are guided by more holistic measures of the common good we share.

The key to a successful Stat implementation is starting and not stopping. And this drive comes directly from the leader.

So *start and don't stop*.

Notes

Notes